DR. JOHN GILL

J. R. Broome

Address given at
the Annual General Meeting of
The Gospel Standard Trust
19 May 1990.

GOSPEL STANDARD TRUST PUBLICATIONS
1991
7 Brackendale Grove, Harpenden,
Herts. AL5 3EL, England

© J. R. Broome 1991

ISBN 0 903556 92 8

Printed in Great Britain
by Flair Press

DR. JOHN GILL

Dr. Gill spent his life in London. He was fifty-one years a pastor of a church in Southwark, and lies buried in Bunhill Fields along with John Bunyan and Isaac Watts. He established his reputation initially through his *Commentary on the Song of Solomon*. He commenced preaching sermons on the Song of Solomon in 1723 when he was 26 and they were published five years later in 1728. He preached them — 122 sermons — on Sunday mornings in his church at Southwark. When they were published they ranked alongside the commentary of James Durham, and through this work he became known in London, this country and the United States. He followed with a second work which became equally famous. It was the result of a series of sermons against the error of Arminianism and was published as a book entitled *The Cause of God and Truth*. This series of sermons was published in four parts between 1735 and 1738. They constitute firstly an answer to texts used by Arminians to support their error, secondly they explain texts used to support the doctrines of grace, and thirdly they refute the arguments used by Arminians. *The Cause of God and Truth* has been republished many times.

But, pre-eminently Gill is known for his *Commentary on the whole Bible*. He published the New Testament part of that Commentary in three volumes between 1746 and 1748. The Old Testament part followed in four volumes between 1763 and 1768. He took twenty-two years from 1746 to 1768 to accomplish this great work. In the last century Dr. Doudney, the Editor of the *Gospel Magazine* and a clergyman in the Anglican Church in Southern Ireland enlisted the help of unemployed Irish youths and republished it in six volumes. Gill published in all, 10,000 folio pages of writing — a vast volume of writing on the Scriptures. The penultimate work of his life was his *Body of Divinity*, published in two volumes in 1769. This he followed in 1770 with his *Body of Practical Divinity* which was the year before he died. He was working right to the end of his life. The *Body of Divinity* is an exposition of the doctrines of Scripture very simply and graciously set forth.

It was a remarkable feature of John Gill that he was self-educated. He never went to university nor received any training other than a few years at a local grammar school in his home town. The reason for this was that the headmaster of his school favoured the Anglican church and forced his pupils to attend. Gill coming from a Particular Baptist home in Kettering declined to go, and therefore had to leave the Grammar School at the age of 16. In 1748 at the age of 51, when he published his New Testament Commentary, the University of Aberdeen recognised the Rabbinical scholarship which it contained, and awarded him a Doctorate of Divinity on the strength of the first volumes. He had taught himself Hebrew and became in his day one of the greatest, if not *the* greatest, Hebrew scholar of his time. He was equally self-taught in Greek and Latin. Mr. Philpot, who had a 'double first' from Oxford in Greek and Latin says, "Gill was a most indefatigable student and a thoroughly good scholar," and adds, "He is confessedly very great." This is high praise from J. C. Philpot, who conserved his praise for nothing but the best.

Gill lived in London in the days when Toplady was there. Toplady says, "Certainly no man has treated the momentous subject of Calvinism, the system of divine grace in all its branches more closely and judiciously and successfully than Dr. Gill." Philpot says that the Doctor had a clear head and an able pen. Toplady said of him what was said of the Duke of Marlborough, "He never fought a battle he did not win," and Philpot says that the Arminians had no more chance with the Calvinist Doctor than Marshall Tallard and the French had with the victor of Blenheim.

Added to his scholarship he was also a very godly and deeply taught man. Philpot says he knew the truth. All through his Commentary he never lost sight of it. He believed the Scriptures and that the Scriptures were a consistent, harmonious revelation of the mind and will of God. The Gospel of the grace of God he believed to be the grand key of Old and New Testaments; and this gave his Commentary its great value, so that the Doctor was not a Calvinist on one page and an Arminian on another, building up and pulling down neither consistent with truth nor with himself. Gill explains every passage in his Commentary in conformity with the analogy of faith. He never slips by any hard text without trying to explain it, and "if there is no satisfactory answer," says Philpot, "in Gill's Commentary, we are not likely to find it anywhere else." The Doctor was very candid in acknowledging difficulties. He was a Rabbinical scholar versed in all the writings and customs of the ancient Jews. Philpot says, "he writes in an instructive, edifying and savoury manner." This is high commendation from J. C. Philpot, whose other favourite writer was William Huntington.

Reviewing a reprint of Gill's *Commentary on the Song of Solomon* in 1855, Mr. Philpot has this to say, "As an expositor of Scripture, Gill shines with unrivalled lustre. John Owen's *Commentary on Hebrews* is probably the deepest and greatest ever given to the church, but Gill is more readable, more concise and pregnant, more lively and animated than Owen; if he did not dig so deeply into the mines of heavenly truth nor turn up such massive ore, yet is there dust of gold in all that he lays bare and brings to the light of day. Both Owen and Gill were Masters in Israel, both eminent for natural abilities and acquired learning, both good and great men whose works praise them in the gates and whom successive generations rise up and call blessed." It is of interest that Owen was Chancellor of Oxford University in the days of Oliver Cromwell. It is equally interesting that J. C. Philpot should have equated these two godly men, considering that Gill had only those few years' education up to the age of sixteen.

Gill is undoubtedly the greatest Particular Baptist theologian. We cannot find amongst our forebears a greater than Dr. Gill. He was sound in all the doctrines of the faith. We can point to men who were sound to a point, such as Richard Baxter, but were at variance with truth in other places. When we come to Dr. Gill we find a man thoroughly sound in the Scriptures, thoroughly sound in the doctrine of the Trinity, thoroughly sound in the sovereign decrees of God, the fall, redemption, justification, regeneration, sanctification and final perseverence. Gill is abundantly clear about such things as conditional faith and the point of justification, and doctrinally stands closely in agreement with our Gospel Standard Articles of Faith; more closely than with the 1689 Particular Baptist Confession of Faith. The only major difference where he differs from our Articles of Faith, is that he accepted the Law as the believer's rule of life. But he did not do that in a legalistic manner.

As regards the preaching of the Gospel, Gill is clear. (You might remember that there were men in London at the time like Isaac Watts, Joseph Hart, and others.) He says in his *Body of Divinity*, "The Gospel is not an offer but a preaching of Christ crucified," and how our heart echoes that. One of the words the Lord spoke to our heart before we went into the ministry was this, "*Preach the Word,*" and we have seen a great glory in it. We see it here with Dr. Gill, "The Gospel is not an offer but a *preaching* of Christ crucified, a proclamation of the unsearchable riches of His grace, of peace, pardon, righteousness and life and salvation by Him." He goes on to say, "Nor is the Gospel ministry an offer of Christ and of His grace and salvation by Him which are not in the power of the minister of it to give, nor carnal man to receive." Speaking of the external call of the Gospel, "Many are called but few are chosen," he says, "The external call may be considered as a call to sinners in a state of nature and unregeneracy, but it is not a call to them to regenerate or convert themselves, of which there is no instance in the Bible, and which is the pure work of the Holy Spirit of God, nor to make their peace with God which they cannot make by anything they can do and which is only made by the blood of Christ. Nor is it a call to get an interest in Christ which is not got but given, nor to the exercise of evangelical grace such as faith or repentance which they have not, and therefore can never exercise; nor to any spiritual vital acts of which they are incapable, being natural men and dead in trespasses and sins." Regarding faith and repentance, whether they belong to the Gospel or the Law, he wrote this, "Is faith a duty of the moral Law, or is it to be referred to the Gospel? It may be answered that as the Law is not of faith, so faith is not of the Law. As for special faith in Christ as a Saviour or believing in Him to the saving of the soul, this the Law knows nothing of, nor does it make it known." Regarding repentance he wrote, "True repentance is as faith, a blessing of the covenant of grace and so is a doctrine of the Gospel and not of the Law."

Because Gill stands where he does, he has been called the prince of Hypercalvinists. This is what Jack Hoad, referring to him in his recent book *The Baptist*, says, "It was Gill's influence which was the major factor in the retention of a high Calvinistic theology by those Particular Baptist Churches, which holding restricted communion for two centuries after his death came to be known as Strict Baptists." Errol Hulse, in his *Introduction to the Baptists* (1973) says that, "It is noteworthy that Gill's friends were such men as John Skepp and John Brine, both Hypercalvinists." Errol Hulse goes on to say that, "Gill's preference in literature lay in the direction of such men as Tobias Crisp," and he adds "though happily John Owen and Thomas Goodwin were also found in his reading." But one thing is clear with Gill; in his day he had no Arminian friends, he stood separate. Hulse says that, "Gill's failure lay not so much in what he said but in what he omitted to say. . . . Unhappily he restricted the Gospel by failing to beseech the unconverted to be converted to God. To fail to do justice to the Scriptures which highlight man's responsibility to believe and repent, and to suppress the gracious invitations of Christ to all men, is to deprive the word 'Gospel' of its real meaning." It is clear that Gill did this purposely. It was not an oversight, it was a matter of divine teaching. He saw the solemn error of man-made exhortations. He saw the blessed commission, "*Preach* the Word," and that included preaching, presenting, proclaiming, but it did not include offering. The Holy Spirit's anointing of the Word drew sinners to Christ and that clearly is the position of Dr. Gill. It gives us good reason to say that he stood close to the Gospel Standard Articles of Faith.

He was born at Kettering in 1697. He died at Camberwell, London in 1771 and was buried in Bunhill Fields. He was called by grace at the age of 12 under the text, "Adam, . . . where art thou?" He was blessed, as he says, with 'exceeding great and precious promises,' and came before the church at Kettering on 1 November 1716 at the age of 18. He was received by them and baptized the same day and sat down to the Lord's table on the following Sunday. That same evening, the first day he sat down to the Lord's supper, he attended a Prayer Meeting in a private house, and there he read and expounded the 53rd chapter of the prophecy of Isaiah. The next Sunday, in the same place, he preached from I Corinthians 2. 2, "I determined not to know any thing among you save Jesus Christ, and Him crucified." After preaching for a few occasions he came before the church at Kettering and was sent out by them to preach, and so like the apostle Paul, it was true of him, that having been baptized, he straightaway 'preached Jesus'. He spent a little time at Higham Ferrers, near Northampton, helping another minister to preach in the local villages, and here he married Elizabeth Negus. He always felt that his visit to Higham Ferrers providentially was for that sole reason. She became his devoted partner and died in the year 1764 at the age of 67. They were married for 46 years. They had many children, only three survived them. One girl died at the age of 13 and made a good end. Her funeral sermon was published by him.

He returned from Higham Ferrers for a short while to Kettering, but did not stay there long. Whilst there his ministry was greatly blessed. One of the men who was called by grace under his early ministry was John Brine. He was about 17 at the time. Brine was baptized at Kettering and sent out to preach by the church. He first went to Coventry to take a pastorate, and later moved to Cripplegate in London. Gill and Brine were great friends. Brine was 35 years in London as a pastor and died at the age of 63. He was one of the leading ministers of the Particular Baptists in the eighteenth century and only recently the Gospel Standard Library has been able to purchase his complete works. He lies buried in Bunhill Fields.

In April 1719 Gill received a call to come to London to a church at Horselydown, Fair Street, Southwark; this was just south of Tower Bridge. He preached for two months in April and May and in August and September came again. Eventually he accepted the call to the pastorate and was ordained on 22 March 1720. He was 22 years old when he took up his pastorate. One of the ministers who took part in that ordination service was John Skepp. Skepp was a member of an Independent church at Cambridge under John Hussey, the author of the book *God's Operations of Grace but no Offers of Grace*. Skepp came from Cambridge to London to be minister at the Currier's Hall in Cripplegate. He was a brilliant Hebrew scholar. Here is one of the threads in the chain of divine providence in the life of Gill. On 1 December 1721 Skepp died. He was only 46. All his Rabbinical books, which had come from Cambridge, were left to Gill. Clearly they were the foundation for his New Testament Commentary. He used them and his books exude the learning he obtained from them. Skepp lies buried with Gill in Bunhill Fields. As *his* ministry ended in the capital in 1721 so Gill's began.

Prior to Gill coming to Horselydown they had had a famous pastor. In 1668 Benjamin Keach had become the pastor at Horselydown. He was succeeded by his nephew Benjamin Stinton. Stinton is an interesting man. He had made a collection of the documents relating to the history of the Particular Baptists, running through the end of the 17th century and on into the 18th century. That was the series of documents which Thomas Crosby used to produce his *History of the English Baptists*. Thomas Crosby was one of Gill's deacons at Horselydown. When Gill succeeded Stinton it was the pastorate for a life's work. The church moved to a new building in Carter's Lane, Tooley Street in 1757. Gill was there until his death in 1771. He exerted not only in London but in England a profound influence. When he died in 1771 he was succeeded by Dr. Rippon, famous for his *Hymnal* and his *Baptist Register*. Rippon became pastor in 1773 and he stayed until 1836. It was in his time that the church moved to New Park Street, and it was to this church that C. H. Spurgeon received his call in 1854. He stayed as pastor until 1892 during which time it moved to the Metropolitan Tabernacle. So there is a continuity in this church of Keach, Stinton, Gill, Rippon and Spurgeon, and the church moving from Horsleydown, to Carter's Lane, to New Park Street, and to the Metropolitan Tabernacle.

It is clear that whilst Spurgeon often used to say he wished in his days to revive the doctrine and teaching of Gill, there were major differences between them. Spurgeon in his ministry condemned what he termed Hypercalvinism, and therefore condemned Gill. He did say however, "For good, sound, sober, massive common sense in commentating who can excel Gill." And Spurgeon went on to say of his *Song of Solomon*, "The best thing that Gill ever did, the work is very precious." But equally, Spurgeon says in his *Commenting and Commentaries*, "Gill is one-sided. He is the Coryphaeus — the leader — of Hypercalvinists."

Some years ago at the annual lecture at the Evangelical Library, Dr. Martyn Lloyd-Jones was in the chair when the subject was Dr. Gill. He had this to say, "I am indebted to John Gill, in particular among his various works that have been mentioned this evening for that volume *The Cause of God and Truth*. How faithfully it answers the many texts that are often used by Arminians to prove their error." But like Spurgeon Dr. Lloyd-Jones considered Gill to be a Hypercalvinist.

So we come to our assessment of Gill. He is *the* principal predecessor of our position among the Particular Baptists in the 18th century. Hussey, Skepp, Gill, Brine, Huntington are all clearly united around the truths of our Gospel Standard position, and our feeling is that we could possibly include Toplady and Romaine close to that position. The offer, duty faith and duty repentance are found in the Canons of Dort, the Westminster Confession of Faith and in the Particular Baptist Confessions of 1677 and 1689. Jack Hoad says in his book on *The Baptists*, "Gill's stern preaching style shaped the character of preaching among these Particular Baptists, termed Strict Baptists for two centuries after his death. His influence was a major factor in the retention of the high Calvinist theology of a substantial part of these churches."

Hypercalvinism is a false epithet. It is the epithet used by offer ministers to describe those who truly *preach* the gospel and do not exceed the divine commandment, "Go into all the world and *preach* the gospel." The emphasis is there, *"preach."* Gill drew back from the halfway house of semi-Arminianism and we need to know our ground today. We are constantly maligned as Hypercalvinists and we need to stand unashamedly in the position where Gill, Brine, Huntington, Gadsby, Warburton, Kershaw, MacKenzie, Tiptaft, Philpot, Joseph Hatton, J. K. Popham and J. H. Gosden stood firmly in their day. Let us not be ashamed to stand where our great and godly forebears stood to maintain the truth, "as the truth is in Jesus." Anything less is the halfway house to Arminianism. A classic example of what happens is in the Missionary Society founded under the Secretaryship of Andrew Fuller who wrote the book *The Gospel Worthy of all Acceptation.* He was the great exponent of the offer and duty faith and the great opponent of William Gadsby. That Baptist Missionary Society has become Arminian. Let us not taint the truth with tinges of Arminianism. Let us stand clearly for the gospel of the free grace of God as Toplady and John Warburton stood. Warburton, on the second page of his *Mercies of a Covenant God* says this, "I was given up to all manner of wickedness and so continued until my arrival at that time and place which God had purposed, not to offer but to call by grace: 'To change the heart, renew the will, and turn the feet to Zion's hill.' "

Gill's *Body of Divinity* is in print today. It contains a concise statement of all the truths most surely believed among us. Equally his great Commentary is in print today and can be obtained in this country; also his book *The Cause of God and Truth* is obtainable. We should do well to read the works of this godly man. There is no question, he is one of the founders of the Gospel Standard denomination, and stands with J. C. Philpot and J. K. Popham as one of our great theologians.